Cripples' Home, Bray, Co. Dublin.

AN ADDRESS

BY

MRS. LUCINDA SULLIVAN,

DELIVERED BEFORE THE

British Association for the Advancement of Science,

On Thursday, the 22nd August, 1878,

BEING THE OCCASION OF THEIR VISIT TO THE CRIPPLES' HOME, BRAY.

PUBLISHED BY REQUEST.

DUBLIN:
GEORGE HERBERT, 117 GRAFTON STREET.

1878.

Price Threepence.

ADDRESS.

LADIES AND GENTLEMEN,

I desire to offer you my most grateful thanks for the distinguished honour which you have this day conferred on the Home, and will at once proceed to give you a brief outline of its history, objects, and success.

In a quiet cemetery, not far from here (Kill-'o-the-Grange) there is a simple stone slab with this inscription, "*Thou hast delivered my soul from death, mine eyes from tears, and my feet from falling.*" It marks a cripple's grave. In the prime of life, before he was thirty years of age, he was attacked by tetanus, and for upwards of twenty years he lived a lingering death, being crippled in every joint in his body. When first I saw him, it was in vain that I tried to suppress my emotion, which he observing, said: "Whenever you think of me, let it be as of one to whom God has been very gracious." My first interest in those of crippled limb was then awakened.

Ten years later (1872), my life was saved from imminent peril of shipwreck. Since then it has been my desire to devote that life to the alleviation of human suffering. To this end I spent some time in different foreign hospitals and kindred institutions, learning there how best to nurse the sick. My last stay was at Kaiserswerth on the Rhine, and there I would fain have lingered, and have been instrumental in founding a small hospital for incurables, as a thank-offering to

Almighty God, for deliverance from a watery grave. However, this could not then be accomplished, and I became responsible for the charges of a deserted crippled child who was in the institution, instead. My interest in him was the second step to the Cripples' Home.

Still, it was not until after a residence of two years in the Adelaide Hospital, Dublin, that I became at all aware of how great was the need in Ireland for a Cripples' Home, or of how many little ones, suffering from spinal and joint diseases, pass their miserable lives drifting from one hospital to another, till their sufferings end in death. As a rule, if children when first attacked are brought to hospital, they will derive considerable benefit from some months' treatment, until the kind surgeon, observing the pallor on his young patient's cheek from long confinement, advises a change to the fresh sea air, generous diet, scrupulous care, and cheerful surroundings. It is not an easy task to repeat this charge to some poor mother, herself the picture of want, the very odour from whose threadbare garments only tells too truly how foul the air, how dismal and how damp the abode to which she carries her crippled child. Nor is it a matter for surprise that after a few months the same child lies again upon a bed in the same hospital ward, thinner, and more suffering this time, and again to be dismissed with feebler prospects of recovery than before. And yet, once more, a poor, distorted, shrivelled-up, suffering object is borne up the stairs—every movement agonizes—every footstep tortures—every accent wearies. The low, ceaseless moaning alone tells that life is there, till the messenger of release comes, and the crippled child no longer needs our care. I do not paint from imagination ; I tell you facts. Scenes, such as I have described, are being enacted in all large cities, and will continue to be enacted wherever a Cripples' Home does not exist.

Those among the wealthier classes who have similar sufferers in their own households know well the amount of care which such cases require, but none among us can know how deep the misery of the poor, when deformity, pain, and helplessness are added to their other privations. Then, indeed, is their bitter cup filled to the very brim!

Again, even while under the best hospital treatment, crippled children may well arouse our pity. For weeks or months are they confined to bed, mind free, body bound, their education meanwhile totally neglected, though they are often quite capable of learning, and would be much benefited, physically as well as mentally, by regular lessons. So, while I mourned over them, I often longed for what then, indeed, seemed an impossibility—namely, that school life, such as delicate children are capable of, might be combined with hospital care and treatment. And I also thought how during those long, listless hours through which the cripples passed, some suitable handicraft might well be acquired, which would form a pleasing and healthy distraction from pain or study, and which would enable the cripple hereafter to earn a subsistence. Hospital care, school training, industrial occupation. These three, how I longed to see them combined! But to have them combined in a pleasant country home, among the green fields, near the sparkling sea, and with pure, fresh air from breezy heights—this—this, indeed, became to me a dream-land, where all my thoughts, whether waking or sleeping, centred. And ever, as some emaciated little one, once so patient and so dear, now so still and cold, was removed from my charge, the bitter cry of a woe still unheeded in our midst, seemed to reverberate through my very soul! I had mourned over them, I had longed for them, but now I formed *plans* respecting them. Silence had become an impossibility, and I spread the cripples' need before all with whom I came in contact. None turned a deaf ear—none denied the facts, or questioned the desirability of establishing such a home, but I failed to find one who would undertake the initiative. Many promised support, many sympathised and spoke words of encouragement; all said *they* could do no more. Then, when every other help failed, I cast myself and the burden of the cripples' need upon Him who faileth not, and I rose from my knees with my plans merged into the strong *resolve* to undertake the work myself in the strength of God, and to say, with one of old, "In the name of Jesus of Nazareth, rise up and walk." Not, indeed, but that at the time this seemed almost impossible. My health was then indifferent, my time was entirely occupied, and I had not one penny in hand for the purpose. Still, that mighty Voice, whose slightest accents may never lightly be disregarded, had spoken to my soul, and on the 23rd of October, 1874, I wrote the following letter :—

HOME FOR CRIPPLED CHILDREN.

To the Editor of the DAILY EXPRESS.

SIR,—I think I may safely venture to say that the want in Ireland of such an Institution as a Cripples' Home has long been felt by those who are best acquainted with the poor and their necessities—necessities which are doubly aggravated when accompanied by bodily deformity and its consequent suffering, isolation, and helplessness; for it is but seldom that the poor cripple can earn a sufficient subsistence, and too often must he either enduré the pain of being a burden on those whose earnings are scanty enough for their own support, or else pass his weary days within the workhouse walls, as in a living grave. But sad as this may be where adults are concerned, it is still worse as respects the unhappy little ones, who, with deformed bodies, are not unfrequently left with uninstructed minds, looking on wistfully while others play, or lying, it may be, in some foul corner, more like the beasts that perish than immortal beings for whom, as Christians, we are bound to believe that Jesus died.

Oh, for some sweet country home where these inheritors of misfortune might be cared for, loved, instructed, and invigorated!

It is not to be wondered at that these thoughts press forcibly on me at this moment, for a little crippled boy, five years of age, is moving about on the ground at my feet. I cannot say that he creeps along, for his lower limbs are powerless, but he uses his arms like a pair of oars, and thus propels himself. Poor little fellow! He is quite proud of his red shoes, which a lady has given him, and all unconscious of how deeply he is afflicted.

Of another little cripple, about the same age, I had intended saying something, but I need not do so now. He has gone hence—gone at his Saviour's call to the beautiful land, where "the lame shall leap as an hart," and the lips that here uttered only cries of pain, are filled with songs of the glory!

What a contrast to this vision is presented by the emaciated, shrivelled-up figure of a boy lying on a bed at a little distance. Though only twelve years old there is in the pale face that indescribable look of age, which is the sure footprint of suffering, and cannot fail to startle the beholder. Four years ago he was in the same hospital with hip disease, and had he been placed under favourable circumstances when he was then removed, his limb would (in the opinion of the surgeon who attended him) have regained its soundness. But what with foul air, unwholesome and insufficient diet, and no means of supplying the needed rest, the efforts of nature towards recovery were thwarted, and not long since he had to be carried into the same ward again, with the disease so far advanced, that nothing short of excision of the joint could avail to save his life. "Safe in the arms of Jesus," he whispered, just before he underwent the operation, and the same sweet words have been often on his lips since then. Surely, few have ever more needed their comfort? His mother, after seven years of widowhood, entered Hospital the same week as he did. She was worn out with long struggling and watchings, and died three days after, leaving five orphan children, only two of whom are old enough to earn for themselves. What was to become of the homeless, motherless, crippled boy? Rather, who would not have said with me—"I will take the suffering child to my heart, and care for him myself"? But why should only one be saved? There are many, many more equally suffering, equally destitute. Dear reader, if the love of God has any place in your soul, I ask you not to let them perish. Let us start a Cripples' Home. Let us do it in faith. The Lord has done great things elsewhere. Is He not the same prayer-hearing God in Ireland? Let us only trust Him, and go forward in His Name, and He will surely bless us.

It has been calculated that the number of cripples in England and Wales alone is not less than 100,000. I do not know how many cripples we have in Ireland; but bearing in mind the fact that poverty and drunkenness are the fruitful sources of countless evils to helpless infants, one can hardly suppose our number to be below the average in the sister land. In England there are now at least three Homes for Cripples. Ireland has, as yet, not one. Still the voice of the impotent man, so long vainly waiting for mercy, ascends to the ear of his God, as he cries, "I have no man to help me, but while I am coming another steppeth down before me." Yes, for almost every other form of human misery some shelter has been provided, but the cripple shivers still in loneliness and neglect.

But some may say, "We have enough of charitable institutions already; why add another?" To such I fearlessly reply, "We have still one too few while we lack a Cripples' Home."

The suitable and commodious building recently known as "The Bray Auxiliary to the Hospital for Incurables" has been kindly lent for the purpose of a Cripples' Home. And now I plead for further help. An empty house is not much to start with. But I should be wanting in grateful memory of the past, if I did not know full well that help, true, liberal, and loving help, will not be slow to come.

One word as to the working and principles of the Institution, and I have done. Children under twelve years of age will be received from all parts of Ireland as funds and space will allow. Misery will be the chief title to admission, and that without respect of creed. The children will be trained with a view to ultimate self-support. The fundamental principle of the Institution will be this—Every inmate must receive religious instruction direct from the Word of God.

I remain, Sir, yours faithfully,

LUCINDA SULLIVAN.

CHILDREN'S SURGICAL WARD,
ADELAIDE HOSPITAL, DUBLIN.
Oct. 23rd, 1874.

The letter appeared on the 26th, and also an able editorial article on the subject. The Home is deeply indebted to Mr. Robinson, and to his untiring advocacy I feel that much of its success is due. The editors of our other leading papers have also shown uniform kindness. May God bless them all, and make them a power for good in our land!

Such was the *origin* of the Cripples' Home.

With respect to its *success*. I had been calculating the probable preliminary expenditure, and felt that I might safely start the Home whenever I should have the sum of £300 for the purpose. The letter appeared on a Tuesday morning, and by the following Saturday I had received exactly £300, while by December 31st I had received £1000, and had lodged the greater part of it in the Royal Bank, to the credit of the Cripples' Home. *It all came in answer to that one letter.* The first large donation was the sum of £100 from Mrs. Charles Pease, quickly followed by £50 from James Tyrrell, Esq. The late Lieut. Armar Lowry was also one of the first and best friends of the Home. He gave £100 towards an investment fund, to which his brother, Lieut. John Lowry, added £50. More recently, the late Colonel the Right Hon. W. F. F. Tighe, augmented this fund by a donation of £300. This was (with a single exception), the largest gift received yet from a single individual, and, perhaps, as Colonel Tighe's footsteps are no longer on earth, I may be pardoned for adding, that while in the letter which accompanied his donation, he expressed the warmest interest in the work, he wished that no public acknowledgment should be made of it, only a prayer offered on his behalf as a sufficient return. His works do follow him. The other principal donors to the Home have been Miss Margaret Fetherston; Lady Napier; Mrs. Henry Sherrard; the late Harriett Lady Verner; the Misses Brooke, per J. Richardson, Esq.; E. A. S., in memoriam; Mrs. Thompson; H., per G. R. Wade, Esq.; and the late Miss Maria Pringle, who bequeathed to it £300.*

At the same time, it is but right and just to add, that had it not been for the smaller offerings of the many, in addition

* The largest Annual Subscribers to the Home are—Mrs. P. C. Crampton, Mrs. Arthur Hornby, Miss Margaret Fetherston, Lady Olive Guinness, Lady Inchiquin, Miss C. Fetherstonhaugh, Miss La Nauze, The Most Noble the Marquis of Conyngham, In Memoriam (J. H. Frawley), St. Matthias's Church Saturday Class, Rutland Square Church Ladies' Sewing Meeting, Mariners' Church, Kingstown, and Miss Smyth's Class, St. Matthias's.

to the larger ones of the few, the work could never have progressed as it has done.

But it is not in money only that sympathy has been expressed, and help has come for the Home. For many months the average number of letters received and answered was from fifteen to twenty per day; some from the very poor, enclosing, perhaps, a shilling's worth of stamps; some from sick and weary ones, whose own suffering had taught them to feel for those similarly afflicted, and who offered the best and most precious, as well as the most prevailing of all offerings, even their prayers.

Many of these letters were well calculated to touch the tenderest sympathies of our nature. I will only mention one of them. It was from a clergyman's wife, and contained one pound. The writer said, "The £1 which I enclose for your proposed Cripples' Home, was earned by a talented son, now with his Heavenly Father, and found in his pocket after his death. It has lain by since then, as I never could bring myself to spend it, but your appeal has so touched my heart, that I send it to you for the Cripples' Home, and may God bless the undertaking! The moment that note reached me, I felt certain that God would make it the seed of an abundant harvest, and so it proved.

The Home has been rich, indeed, in sympathising friends! First and foremost among these the name of that august lady, Her Grace the Duchess of Abercorn, must ever be held in grateful recollection. By tenderest interest, and words of strong encouragement, she helped me on. Her own sympathies were keenly alive to the need for a Cripples' Home in Ireland; and while I was mourning over it in a pent-up hospital ward, her Grace (though in far different surroundings), often pondered on the same thing, and longed also for a Cripples' Home. By repeated visits, by liberal donation, by bon-bons laid aside for the little cripples when the Castle's festive board was spread; by scrap-books made with her own hands during hours of weakness in another land; by frequent letters; by flowers gathered for her own use in the Viceregal gardens, but brought here by herself to adorn the Home, and finally, by laying the foundation stone of this Hall in which we meet, and which bears her Grace's name, was that interest expressed, and since leaving our shores she has written to say that she "will never forget this her favourite Home in Ireland." The odour of the roses which she brought has died away, but the memory of her goodness cannot die, and I trust that while the Cripples' Home exists, the title, "Duchess of Abercorn" may remain inscribed upon its walls. Nor has her Grace the Duchess of Marlborough shown a less lively interest in its welfare; and on Monday last, I had, for the second time, the honour of conducting her through the Home, to which she generously contributed, and with which she was pleased to express very great satisfaction.

But it is as respects the children themselves that the success of the Home has been most marked. There has been but one death within its walls, and that was in the case of a little girl, near her last moments, who so longed to be brought here that, in compliance with her mother's request, she was received. She was released from her sufferings three days later. I was glad she came, that the other children, and all who ministered to her, might learn from her example, how easy a thing it is to die when we are trusting in Him who has given Himself the endearing title of "The Good Shepherd!"

With this exception, there has been in every case either recovery, or progress towards it. Some who came to die, have remained to live. One of the first inmates (the lad mentioned in the letter), is now earning his own bread in Dublin, and can walk as far as most of us, and that without the aid of crutches. Another, who was partially paralysed and had hip disease in both limbs, has regained his locomotive powers. One little boy, seven years of age, who never walked before, has within the last two months learned to get about with the aid of crutches. Here I would desire to express my gratitude to Dr. Whistler for his gratuitous and valuable services to the Home.

All have (as already said) improved, and that not in health only, but also in disposition, in cheerfulness, and in capacity for, usefulness. Cripples who come here supposing themselves to be helpless, soon discover that they can be helpful, and this new-born joy is to them a spring of healthfulness. The Home is kept, as you see it, principally by the crippled children themselves. They make their beds, dust the rooms, wash up delft, clean the boots, mind their little gardens, and perform all light household duties. The elder cripples care for and tend the younger ones, and this they do right well and lovingly. Believing in the educational power of bright, clean, and instructive surroundings, there are words of Holy Writ and suggestive pictures everywhere. Mr. Gladstone, who visited the Home last autumn, expressed his concurrence in this view, and his pleasure at seeing it carried out in the Home. My expectation is, that the children who have been trained here will, when they leave the Home, bring their love for order and beauty with them, and not their love for them only, but the power of reproducing them, as these things are within the grasp of the poorest in our land. Fairly good prints are now to be had for a nominal price, wild flowers, fern leaves, are within the reach of all, and whitewash, soap, and water are not expensive or unattainable things. Still, we want more of them in almost all our institutions and the dwellings of the poor.

The crippled children are by nature fearful and timid, but are quickly taught the art of being brave; brave to endeavour and brave to endure, and that to encounter a toss without a tear is a virtue worthy of reward.

The average number of inmates from the first has been 14. This is all there was accommodation for till last March, when the new wing, just erected, was ready for occupation. There are at present 20 in the Home, and admittance in course of time has been promised to others. There are numerous applications, but in the interests of the cripples already under my charge, I only admit by degrees. The Home has capacities for 40 inmates, and I do not wish for any increase in that number here, but would like to see, at least, one Home in every province in Ireland. The new wing, completed on the 29th of last November, and opened for the admission of inmates last March, is by far the largest part of the building, and contains 13 rooms. It cost £3,000—plumber's work, architect's fees, and furnishing included. The ground has been purchased in fee-simple, and the building stands rent free for ever. The dormitory in the older part of the Home is called the "Crampton Ward," in memory of the late Judge Crampton, who was principally instrumental in its erection, for the purpose of a temperance hall. But, as this did not succeed, its use has been transferred by the trustees for the Cripples' Home, principally through the kindness of Mrs. P. C. Crampton and T. Lefroy, Esq., Q.C. The Home is conducted on the strictest temperance principles. No stimulants are administered, and the children are enrolled on entrance as members of the Band of Hope. The age for receiving cripples is limited to 12 years, but I prefer younger children, as there is more hope of doing them permanent good. There is no limit as to the length of time which a cripple shall be kept, except this—till they can earn a subsistence, or be otherwise provided for. I would rather confer a real and lasting benefit on a few than a partial benefit on many. I believe that every institution should have a special place for united prayer, and also suitable provision for separating its inmates in case of infectious disease. This room, in which we are this day assembled, is used for the former purpose, and I trust, also, in the course of time, to be able to build a small infirmary in the rere for the latter. Donors of £100 and upwards have their names inscribed over a bed, but this does not confer any right of nomination. Admission is not procured by payments of any kind, votes, or interest, only by the deepest necessity. I conceive that it must be very pleasing to *Him* who laid aside His glory, and laid down His life for us, when the rich strip themselves of their wealth, "hoping for nothing again," and when the neediest finds the readiest entrance to a Home founded in His name. And I must gratefully add that the help has never failed. And, although entirely dependent on voluntary support, from day to day, no monetary anxiety has ever troubled my mind; neither want nor debt have ever crossed the threshold of the Home, and this may, perhaps, appear the more remarkable when I say that no single individual has ever been solicited for help.

I have trusted God Himself to remind His children *when* and *how* to help the Home *as He has helped them,* and have never had reason to depart from this confidence. He has been very gracious, and has inclined the hearts of His people to give far more than any words of mine could have done. I have said that no debt has ever been incurred for the Home. I find it much easier to adapt my wants to the funds in hand, than to incur debt by going beyond them, and I believe it to be a safe principle, that the measure of the help which God sends us, is to be taken as the measure of the work which He means us to do, and when we go beyond that, what we sometimes call faith, may, perhaps, prove after all to have partaken more of the nature of disobedience. Some friends have also said, that I must not expect a continuance of the liberal help given at the first—that many who will contribute to start a charity, will not go on supporting it. But neither has this been my experience. The funds have come in year by year increasingly. Last year's receipts were in excess of all former years, and this year has, for the same period, already exceeded last year. God has, indeed, given me not only what I asked, but exceedingly above all I asked or thought. And ever as I look at the crippled limbs of my afflicted charge, I try also to look up to Him whose resources are uncrippled things, and who delights to use the weak things which man despises.

In conclusion, one word with respect to the *object* which I have in view. And what is that? Not the alleviation of human suffering merely, nor the saving of a few lives from helplessness and misery to usefulness and happiness; not even the salvation of their immortal souls, but something greater, loftier still, even this, and nothing short of this—THE GLORY OF THE LORD JESUS CHRIST. In His Name and words, I would say, "Bring in hither the poor, the maimed, and the halt;" and to His immortal and beloved Name I would ascribe all the praise for any good that has been done. My best, my very best, and the whole of it, is but a broken worthless thing; nevertheless, it shall be laid at His wounded feet, and the altar will consecrate the gift!

"I take, O Cross, thy shadow
For my abiding-place;
I ask no other sunshine
Than the sunshine of His Face;
Content to let the world go by,
To know no gain nor loss,
My sinful self, my only shame,
My glory all, the Cross!"

PORTEOUS & GIBBS, Printers, 18 Wicklow Street, Dublin.

www.ingramcontent.com/pod-product-compliance
Lightning Source LLC
LaVergne TN
LVHW052039160826
845678LV00003B/1432

* 9 7 8 0 3 5 3 4 2 9 5 9 8 *